MADELINE
IN AMERICA

and Other Holiday Tales

SCHOLASTIC INC.

New York Toronto London Auckland Sydney
Mexico City New Delhi Hong Kong Buenos Aires

MADELINE

IN AMERICA

and Other Holiday Tales by

LUDWIG BEMELMANS

and JOHN BEMELMANS MARCIANO

Arthur A. Levine Books hardcover edition designed by David Saylor, published by Arthur A. Levine Books, an imprint of Scholastic Press, October 1999.

ISBN 0-590-04306-4

12 11 10 9 8 7 6 5 4 3 2 1   1 2 3 4 5 6/0

Printed in the U.S.A.   40

First Scholastic paperback printing, September 2001

TO MIMI

CONTENTS

PREFACE   9

by John Bemelmans Marciano

MADELINE IN AMERICA   11

THE COUNT AND THE COBBLER   55

A BEMELMANS CHRISTMAS MEMORY   63

by Barbara Bemelmans

SUNSHINE   67

PLACES TO FIND IN THESE STORIES   111

PREFACE

The opening story of this collection, "Madeline in America," began life as "Madeline's Christmas in Texas." During a trip through Texas in the early 1950s, my grandfather met and befriended Stanley Marcus of Neiman Marcus. Also on that trip he went to the legendary King Ranch, the size of which exceeds that of some states.

My grandfather came up with the idea of Madeline's spending a Christmas in Texas. He wrote and made sketches for a full-length book. A truncated version, with a dozen pen and ink drawings, was published in a small booklet given out by Neiman Marcus to their shoppers. But the idea was abandoned in favor of a different Christmas idea (which, unfortunately, was also never fully realized). In keeping with the feel of the other Madeline books, I traveled to Texas and painted the sights that now serve as background. (A list of them appears on page 111.)

"The Count and the Cobbler" first appeared as a two-page comic-strip-style spread in the 1935 Christmas issue of *Harper's Bazaar*, my grandfather's first major magazine publication. He republished it in a collection of short stories, *Small Beer*, not as a comic strip but with one picture, accompanied by text, to a page. Here you see it reimagined again, somewhere between the previous two, and in full color.

My grandfather originally wrote "Sunshine" as a treatment for a musical-comedy vehicle for Frank Sinatra. But it soon took shape as a book in the spirit of Madeline—complete with a benevolent female overseer and the use of a city as a central character. He would do for New York what he had done for Paris with *Madeline*.

The story was originally published in *Good Housekeeping* in 1949, and then a year later as a book, in slightly altered form. Due to the expense of color printing in those days, some of the full-color paintings were reproduced in black and white. For this edition, the original full-color painting of Miss Moore selling umbrellas near the Brooklyn Bridge could not be found, and so I did the best I could to repaint it.

Here, as with "Madeline" and "The Count and the Cobbler," I tried not to slavishly copy details and create a Bemelmans pastiche, but to see through my grandfather's eyes. I hope I did him justice.

—*John Bemelmans Marciano*

MADELINE
IN AMERICA

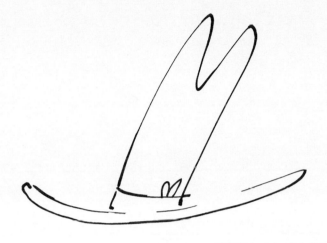

In an old house in Paris

That was covered with vines

Lived twelve little girls in two straight lines,

Including Mademoiselle Madeline Fogg

And Genevieve, her beloved dog.

Two days before Christmas

At half past nine

A cable came for Madeline.

Her great-grandpapa, in bad health,
Had left her all his earthly wealth.
To Dallas Madeline would be sent
For the reading of the last will and testament.

Madeline was sad

At the news of her great-granddad.

The little girls cried, "Boohoo!"

And Miss Clavel said, "We'll all go with you."

In two straight lines they boarded a plane
Because Texas is too far to go by train.
Through the air they flew like a rocket

And were met in Dallas by the lawyer, Crockett.

"Merry Christmas and howdy, ma'am.

The name is Crockett, but call me Sam.

Welcome to Texas, my car's outside.

I'll get you some duds . . .

. . . and we'll go for a ride.

From here on, everything you see,

Miss Madeline, is your property.

This is the mine. It's dark and cold.
But these nuggets here are solid gold.
Now let's get back in the saddle
And take a look at some cattle.

These creatures on the hoof

Seem patient and aloof

But even the most docile breed

Without warning may

S T A M P E D E !

And that helps you to work up a right
Good healthy Texas A P P E T I T E.

This is our cook; his name is Willy;

He turns out a tasty bowl of chili.

Here is what I call a purty sight!"
"Is that an oilfield?" "Yes ma'am, that's right.

Yippiyay! We're just in time to usher
In a million barrel gusher."

"Kind sir, the going's a bit rough.
My little girls have had enough."

"But you have seen nothing. There's one thing more:

I'll take you to the door

Of the world's greatest store!

Miss Madeline, are you aware

That of this store you own a share?"

But now the girls were really dead.
It was time to put each one to bed.
Crockett drove to the hotel.

"Good night, little girls, I hope you sleep well."

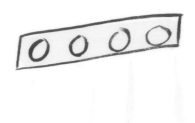

But suddenly Miss Clavel said,
"Oh dear —
Somewhere along the line,
We've lost our little Madeline!"

In Texas, when anyone's in danger,
You call upon the TEXAS RANGER.

"Just give me the facts, ma'am.
I'll do all I can.

WANTED

Yes, ma'am, we're looking everywhere—
By land, by sea, and in the air."

Miss Clavel said, "Oh, dear! I fear
We'll never find her from up here.

But look! Genevieve is pointing below;
Maybe that is the way to go."

And so they park
On the roof, in the dark,
And explore the store
from floor to floor.

Suddenly, things were getting hot.

Madeline was lying on a cot

In a section of the store whereabouts
Was an exhibition of the Girl Scouts.

"Somebody must have locked the door
While Madeline was still in the store.
That closes the case for us, Miss Clavel.
I'll haul you back to your hotel."

The copter left; its taillights were red;
And Madeline was finally put to bed.

"Good morning and merry Christmas to you.
You are not dreaming, all this is true.
We've brought some dresses from the store
For you and your friends and what is more,

Here are the delivery boys
With lots of wonderful dolls and toys.
Enjoy it all while it's here.
Christmas comes but once a year."

"Oh boy, oh joy, this is just fine.
This is the life," said Madeline.
"And there'll be no more school, that is the best part,
For who is rich is already smart."

"You're spoiling my girls and I ask you to stop it,"
Said Miss Clavel to the lawyer, Crockett.
"Don't worry, ma'am—if Madeline could just sit still,
You'd all hear the wisdom of great-grandpapa's will.

It says: 'All my wealth that I give away
Goes to Madeline on her TWENTY-FIRST BIRTHDAY.
Until then, I think it well

That she go back to school with Miss Clavel.'"

To an old house in Paris that was covered with vines
Returned twelve little girls in two straight lines.
In two straight lines they broke their bread
And brushed their teeth and went to bed.

"Good night, dear children, tomorrow we'll talk more
About oil and gold and the world's greatest store.
And now go to sleep and I hope you sleep well."
"Good night, good night, dear Miss Clavel."

Genevieve barked. The stars shone bright.
And Miss Clavel turned off the light.

THE COUNT
AND THE COBBLER

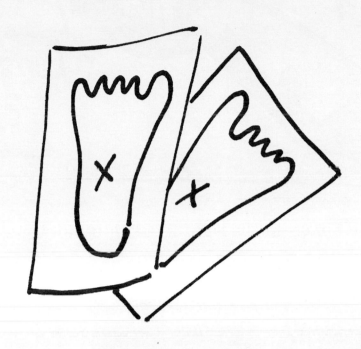

In the little house on the right lived Dominik the cobbler.

He and his wife had many children and little to give them. They were very sad because the children could not go out to sing Christmas carols for they were too poor to buy shoes. It was as the old proverb says: "A cobbler's children are worst shod."

The cobbler was fond of all his children, but most dearly did he love the youngest, a brilliant baby of great talent and promise.

High above the village stood the castle of
Count Cesar de la Tour de la Tour Midi.

The count said to his manservant Joseph, who stood behind his
chair, "We will drive down to the cobbler. I need a pair of shoes."

And they drove down to the village, left the sleigh outside the
house of Dominik the cobbler, and went in to order shoes.

The cobbler took a piece of paper from a stack and thereon traced the feet of Count Cesar de la Tour de la Tour Midi.

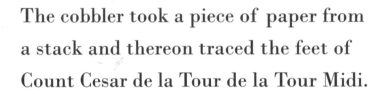

When the cobbler was finished, they went outside and talked about the style of the shoes, the quality and color of the leather, the number of buttons, etc., etc., etc. From inside the house, the cobbler's family watched them through the window, while the brilliant baby made pictures as he had seen his father do.

When the cobbler saw all the pictures
he was very upset, for he did not
know which feet were the count's.

And he worried

and worried

and worried.

Finally he sat down and made all
the shoes, one for each of the drawings.

The night before Christmas, the count came down from his castle,
fished out his shoes, and paid for them. He was so pleased he
ordered another pair, which meant Dominik could afford to buy

a little Christmas tree for his children.

He carried it home

and when it was lit, he gave to each
of his children a pair of the shoes
that the brilliant baby had designed.

And they could go out and sing "Noël-Noël,"
and for once there was a cobbler whose children
were shod.

A BEMELMANS CHRISTMAS MEMORY

by Barbara Bemelmans

My father liked the Christmas season — the cold weather, the snow, the fireplace that burned constantly and into which he put special pine cones that made the flames turn different colors.

My father dressed up as Santa Claus in 1954.

He drew sketches of the sidewalk Santas and took me to the Christmas show at Radio City and to see the tree at Rockefeller Center. He laughed with cab drivers who seemed full of good cheer and smiled back at saluting doormen.

At Luchow's, a restaurant he had gone to since first coming to America, he ate wiener schnitzel and drank beer and chatted in German with the waiters. Listening to the waltzes of Strauss and Schubert, he would grow lonesome for his grandfather's brewery in Regensburg and for the landscape of his childhood Christmases.

There were Christmases spent in hotels—the Irving on Gramercy Park and the Carlyle on Seventy-sixth Street, where Poppy sat on the floor, assembling a set of electric trains for me and then making a papier-mâché tunnel for them to race through. We went to Cuba one year and had a very spare Christmas because Poppy's agent had not sent him the check he promised. Mostly, we went to my grandparents' beautiful white house in Mount Kisco.

The waiters at Luchow's trimming the holiday tree.

I have fond memories of the Christmas eve of 1949. We were sitting at our usual table in "21." Happy people laughed and toasted one another. Poppy had ordered two demitasses and, for me, chocolate ice cream. He lit a cigarette for my mother and an Upmann cigar for himself, and gave me the band to wear as a ring.

Just then, Pete Kriendler, one of the proprietors of "21," shepherded a small flock of navy-uniformed, brass-buttoned Salvation Army volunteers into the festive, wood-paneled room. As he gently guided them from table to table, they brushed against the fur coats of the glamorous, bejeweled, over-coiffed girlfriends and wives of too-rich men. The men thumbed through their wallets and dropped donations in the kettle.

When the little band reached our table, my father smiled and spoke to them in a manner he reserved for those he considered "pure" and "good." I was proud that my beautiful mother was not wearing a fur coat or jewelry, that her hairdo was no more than a few strokes of her own brush, and that she was so much more like those in the navy uniform than like the other women in the room.

It made me happy that the missionaries stayed longest at our table and that, I was certain, my father had given the largest contribution of anyone.

"How sweet. How decent," said my father when the group had gone. Tears glistened in his and my mother's eyes. Arm in arm we walked to Fifth Avenue. Two blocks away, Cardinal Spellman was getting ready to say midnight Mass at St. Patrick's. Poppy hailed a cab.

—Barbara Bemelmans

SUNSHINE

The boy has a poodle, the girl a setter,
And Mr. Sunshine is mailing a letter.
The letter contains the text of an ad
Saying an apartment is to be had.

TWO CHEERFUL ROOMS with bath in a building that truly hath atmosphere and old world charm: in summer cool, in winter warm, venetian blinds, open fireplace, cross ventilation, ample closet space, refrigerator and hardwood floor. A lovely view. Bus stops at door.

But the ceiling sagged and the hall was dark
At two hundred and three Gramercy Park.
Mr. Sunshine hung up a sign and fell
Asleep until someone rang his bell.

He got up from his soft seat
And rushed out into the street.
"Go," he said with angry face.
"Go, look for some other place!
"I don't permit cats or doggies,
People who have noisy hobbies,
People with perambulators,
People who keep alligators,

Artists, acrobats, or players,
Traveling salesman or soothsayers.
To all those and sundry I say
Thank you kindly, go away!"
And so for evident reasons,
For several long seasons,
The apartment at two hundred and three
Was free of any tenantry.

At last a feeble lady's voice
Inquired whether there was any noise
Or commotion in the neighborhood,
And when he said, "No,"
She said, "Very good."
And that she'd be there to see
The charming apartment at half-past three.

As Sunshine stood watching the clock
A sweet old lady came down the block.
"Punctual," he said. "Right on the dot.
In a woman that means an awful lot!
Bless me," said Sunshine, "here advances
A lady in comfortable circumstances.
An unattached female who pays the rent
Year in, year out, to the last cent.
Here comes indeed the perfect tenant—
Perhaps a Mayflower descendant."

In front of the house she stooped and bent low.
With a small whiskbroom she cleared the snow.
And then she fed the pigeons and starlings
And all her other feathered darlings.

Quietly as a mouse
She came into the house.
"Oh," she said, "it's a perfect delight,
It's awfully homey, it's just right.

"It's exactly the kind
Of a place I hoped to find."
"You may have a five-year lease."
"I'm ready to sign it, if you please.

And here is a check
For the first month's rent."
"Dear Madam," said Sunshine,
"You're heaven-sent."

He did not know—
the poor fool—

That Miss Moore was running a music school.

And here we see how Sunshine likes

To be awakened by "The Stars and Stripes."

He dressed in haste and almost fell

Downstairs to the strains of . . .

. . . WILLIAM TELL!

Miss Moore was totally immersed
In music whenever she rehearsed.
"I advise you," said Sunshine, "to desist and cease,
"Or I shall be forced to cancel your lease."

She simply said: "Children—give it all you've got!"
"I'm a patient man—I stand for a lot!
But madam," he said, "this is the last straw.
I shall see you in a court of law."

And after making all that fuss
He ran to catch the Fifth Avenue bus.

He rushed to his lawyer and said: "George, will you please
Thoroughly examine this lease.
And tell me how I can best
Rid myself of this awful pest."

The lawyer took his time and said:
"Sunshine, I'm very much afraid
This is a perfectly good lease.
Music does not disturb the peace.
This unhappy hour,
You underestimated the power
Of a woman
Whom no judge would dare summon.
My advice is: in your place
I would make up my mind to face
The music, and if things don't improve
I counsel you to pack and move."

Sunshine tried hard for a while
To find another domicile.
And he discovered that it was true
That rents were high and places few.

Here we behold the mean old grouch
Trying to sleep on his office couch.

Miss Moore felt fine in the early hours

Although the radio prophesied showers.

She exclaimed: "Upon my soul

I've never owned a parasol!"

She finished her crumpet and then she drank

A second cup of tea and went to the bank.

She drew enough money for the rent

And an additional sum to be spent

For a varied assortment

Of prizes for good deportment.

The sky turned suddenly gray
As Miss Moore was on her way,
And the rain began to fall
As she came to an auctioneer's hall.

Inside the hall a fellow
Held up an antique umbrella.
And the voice of the auctioneer
Bellowed: "Please let me hear
If any of you ladies and gents
Will offer me ten cents."
Miss Moore raised her right hand
And the man on the auction stand
Shouted: "Going, going, gone!
Sold to the lady who stands there alone."

Miss Moore paid
And said,

"Thank you so much.
I had no idea that such
Bargains were still to be had.
I'll be more than glad
To send a lot more
People to your lovely store.
And now I'll bid you good day."

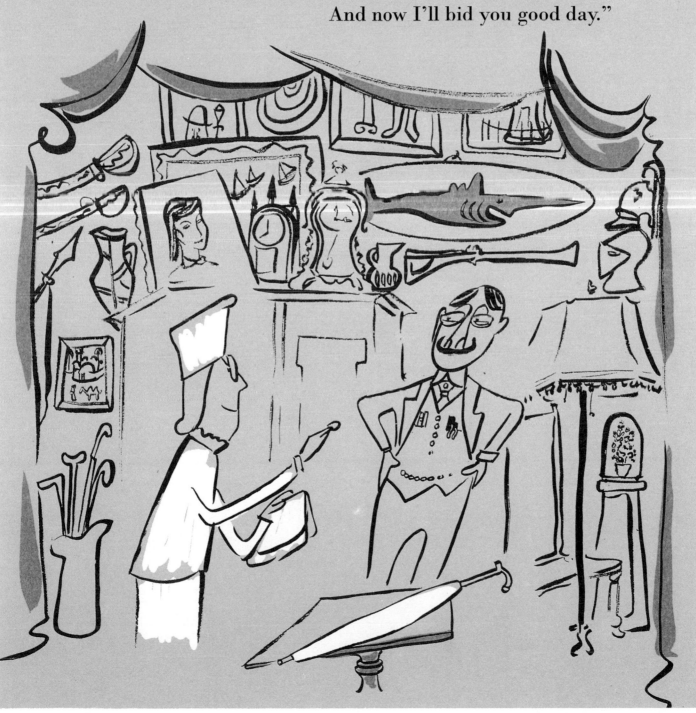

But he said: "There's a balance you have to pay."

"Young man, explain that to me please."

"They're two thousand umbrellas, at ten cents apiece.

They've been lost or found and have gone astray

On the trains and stations of Manhattan's subway."

"Oh, dear," said Miss Moore. "This just about

Leaves me flat—it cleans me out."

"I'm sorry, dear lady. All I can say

Is, you bid for the lot and you have to pay."

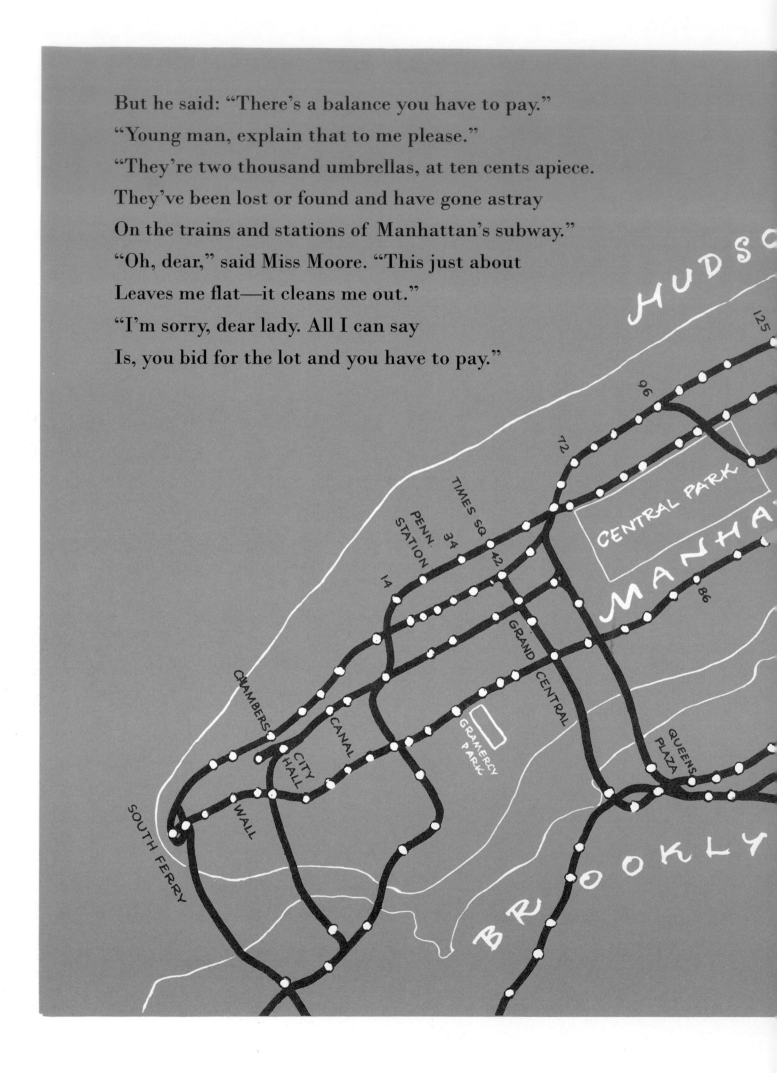

And so that afternoon came a truck

And everyone on the block

Said, "Poor

Miss Moore."

And the neighborhood gossip, a woman named Hattie,

Observed: "The old girl must have gone batty."

Miss Moore was totally immersed
In umbrellas and music as she rehearsed.

Sunshine said: "I'm glad at last to see
You up the proverbial tree.
I'm happy, Miss Moore, to let you know
That the game is up and out you go.
You came here under false pretenses—
I must have been out of my senses.
This will teach me a lesson I'll not forget.
Pack up now, for this place is to let.

"Get out with your doggies and with your cats,
Go rid my house of these noisy brats."
Miss Moore just tapped with her baton
And said, "In a moment, children, we'll go on.
My little friends, I'm very sorry.

"Please don't any of you worry.
We shall simply wait for rain
And sell the old umbrellas again.
We shall continue to occupy this place;
The law gives us a few days' grace.
With the Lord's help, we'll soon send
Mr. Sunshine his overdue rent.
Sunshine, Sunshine go away
And come again some other day!"

In answer to the powerful prayers
Of the son of an Irish cop,

The sun was blotted out by layers
Of clouds, and the sky gave up.

Drainpipes gurgled, gutters choked,
And the citizenry was soaked.

The children left the house as the rain
Came down like out of a water main.

Rusty Regan took pity
On the Mayor's reception committee.

This customer is a United Nations delegate;
The tall building is called the Empire State.

And sold umbrellas to Brooklynites.

It was windy, cold, and showery,
On the Staten Island ferry.

The last umbrella was sold in Astoria
To a visitor who flew in from Peoria.

After the downpour, Miss Moore
Suddenly was no longer poor.
There was no more worry about the rent,
And each child got a new instrument.

They played in Central Park's mall
And gave a concert in Carnegie Hall.

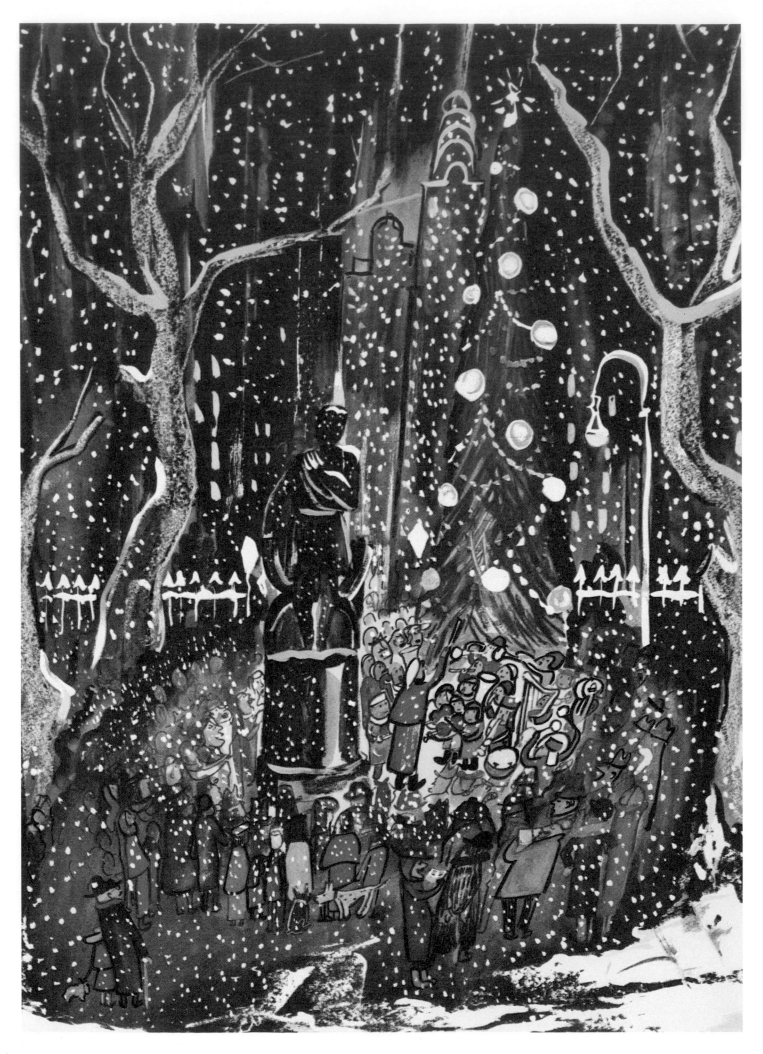

And as the tree was lit up in the dark,
They celebrated Christmas in Gramercy Park.

O ho-ly night!_____ the stars are bright-ly shin-ing, It is the night of the dear Sav-iour's birth; Long lay the world_____ in sin and er-ror pin-ing, Till He ap-pear'd, and the soul felt its worth. A thrill of hope the wear-y world re-joi-ces, For yon-der breaks a new and glo-rious morn._____ Fall_____ on your knees!_____ O hear_____ the an-gel voi-ces! O night_____ di-vine!_____ O night_____ when Christ was born,_____ O night_____ di-vine!_____ O night, O night di-vine!

Late that night came a man to the house.
He muttered he was Santa Claus.

"You'll never guess," he said, "who this is!
I just came to wish you a Merry Christmas.
And tell you that I feel like a heel—
For months I haven't enjoyed a meal.
And the thing that mostly grates me—
Is that my own lawyer hates me.
But," pleaded Sunshine, "if only I could
Come back to this lovely neighborhood—
I like doggies, birds, and cats;
Oh, I'll even put up with rats.
I've become immune to noises,
I love little children's voices,
And I certainly take no exception
To concerts and musical selections."
And so Miss Moore smiled quietly and told
Mr. Sunshine to come in out of the cold.
He thanked her as he knocked the sleet
And snow from his frozen feet.
The cat sat on his lap and purred with mirth,
The dog lay at his feet, and peace was on earth.

PLACES TO FIND IN THESE STORIES

Here is a list of some famous landmarks that appear in these stories:

MADELINE IN AMERICA

Behind the old house in Paris you
can see the
EIFFEL TOWER

Mr. Crockett drives the girls in his
long car past the
TEXAS STATE CAPITAL BUILDING

Madeline and the girls take a
break at the
KING RANCH

On the way to the world's greatest
store they pass
THE ALAMO

Looking for Madeline, Miss Clavel
and Genevieve fly over the
TEXAS STAR,
the largest Ferris wheel in North
America

From the helicopter you can see
the Pegasus sign atop the
MAGNOLIA BUILDING
(formerly called the Mobil
Building)

SUNSHINE

New York City Landmarks

Opposite the first page is
THE SOLDIERS' AND SAILORS'
MONUMENT

Behind the Fifth Avenue bus
stands the
FLATIRON BUILDING

The lady with the baby in the
carriage looks up at the clouds in
front of the
LITTLE CHURCH AROUND THE
CORNER and the
CHRYSLER BUILDING

Behind the citizenry getting
soaked is
GRANT'S TOMB on the left,
RIVERSIDE CHURCH on the right,
with
THE GEORGE WASHINGTON
BRIDGE
in the background

The Mayor's reception committee
stands in front of
CITY HALL

Behind the United Nations
delegate is the
EMPIRE STATE BUILDING

Brooklyn Heights is near
THE BROOKLYN BRIDGE

A visitor from Peoria lands at
LAGUARDIA AIRPORT

From the window of the bank you
can see the arch in
WASHINGTON SQUARE PARK

The children give a concert in
CARNEGIE HALL

This book was designed and art directed by David Saylor. The art for both the jacket and the interior was created using gouache paint. The artwork for Madeline in America *began with Ludwig Bemelmans's pencil sketches. From these, John Marciano recreated the characters in full-color gouache, adding the Texas backgrounds and landmarks in his grandfather's tradition. The art for* The Count and the Cobbler *was rendered in full-color ink by Ludwig Bemelmans, and John recreated them in gouache for this edition, adding two original pieces: the illustration of the cobbler looking out of his door on the bottom of page 57 and the illustration of the cobbler measuring the Count's foot on the top right hand corner of page 58. Ludwig Bemelmans's original art for* Sunshine *was lost, but recreated in full-color for this book by photographing the pages from collectors' editions. For this story, two new pieces of art were added: the illustration of the Brooklyn Bridge on pages 100–101 and the spot of* Sunshine *on page 107. The title page illustration is a reproduction of the 1955 cover that Neiman Marcus used for what they called "The Neiman Marcus Christmas Book." To complete* Madeline in America and Other Holiday Tales, *John created new, original artwork for the title pages, jacket, and spine area of the binding. Three of Ludwig Bemelmans's original sketches for* Madeline in America, The Count and the Cobbler, *and* Sunshine *are featured on the back of the dust jacket. The text was set in 16-point Monotype Bodoni Book, a postscript font based on type designs created in 1798 by Giambattista Bodoni, and redrawn by the Monotype Type Drawing Office in 1921.*